Guide to Git

Practical Guide

A. De Quattro

Copyright © 2024

Practical Guide

1. Introduction to Git

Git is one of the most popular and widely used version control tools in the software development world. Born out of the need to effectively manage changes to source code, Git is now considered the de facto standard for versioning projects, especially those involving distributed teams or large numbers of collaborators. This document aims to provide a detailed understanding of what Git is, its history, the advantages it offers, its main use cases, installation procedures on various operating systems, and initial configuration.

What is Git?

Git is a distributed version control system (DVCS). Its primary purpose is to keep track of changes made to files over time, allowing developers to collaborate on the same project efficiently. Git stores multiple versions of a project, enabling anyone to view and revert to previous states of the files at any time.

Moreover, Git facilitates the work of distributed teams because each developer has a complete copy of the repository on their local machine.

The main advantages of Git over other version control systems include its speed, distributed architecture, and flexibility with branching and merging. This means that multiple developers can work simultaneously on various versions of a project without risking the integrity of each other's work.

Unlike centralized systems like Subversion (SVN), Git does not require a constant connection to a central server. Each local copy of the repository contains the entire history of the project, which means any operation, such as committing, branching, or merging, can be done locally without waiting for server responses.

In summary, Git is designed to facilitate collaborative development while ensuring high efficiency and flexibility.

History and Development of Git

Git was created in 2005 by Linus Torvalds, the creator of the Linux kernel. The context of its creation lies in a radical change in the version control system used by the Linux project.

Until 2002, Linux kernel development was managed through patches and compressed archives. This system proved problematic for such a large project with hundreds of developers working concurrently. To address this issue, the Linux kernel team began using a commercial version control system called BitKeeper. However, in 2005, the Linux team lost the free license to use BitKeeper, prompting Linus Torvalds to develop his own solution. The required features for the new system included distribution, the capability to handle large projects with numerous contributors, and high performance.

Thus, Git was born. Since its launch, Git has become extremely popular not only among contributors to open-source projects but also within companies and among independent developers. Git is now maintained by a large community of developers and is regularly updated and improved.

Key milestones in Git's history include:

- **2005**: Initial release of Git by Linus Torvalds.

- **2006**: The Git project was handed over to Junio Hamano, who became the main maintainer and released version 1.0.

- **2008**: GitHub was launched, providing a platform that leverages Git to host code repositories and facilitate collaboration.

- **2014**: Git became the most popular version control system in the software development world.

- **Today**: Git is the backbone of millions

of projects, both open-source and corporate, and is integrated into numerous development platforms and tools.

Advantages of Using Git

Git offers several significant advantages over other version control systems:

- **Distributed**: Every user has a complete copy of the repository with the entire history. This allows for offline work and provides the flexibility to perform commits and other operations without a connection to a central server.

- **Speed**: Thanks to its distributed architecture, many Git operations, such as committing, branching, and merging, are extremely fast as they are performed locally without needing to interact with a remote server.

- **Advanced Branch Management**: Git makes it very easy to create and manage branches. This encourages developers to work on new features, bug fixes, or other changes in separate branches, which can then be merged into the main branch once completed.

- **Efficient Change Tracking**: Git uses advanced techniques to monitor and record differences between file versions. This allows for precise control over what changes have been made and by whom, making code review simpler.

- **Security**: Git is designed to be secure. Every change in the repository is recorded with a cryptographic hash (SHA-1), ensuring integrity and preventing unauthorized modifications to the project history.

- **Support for Collaborative Work**: Git supports multiple collaborative workflows. Developers can share their work with others through platforms like GitHub, GitLab, or

Bitbucket, which offer interfaces for managing code and pull requests (merge requests).

- **Easy Rollback**: Since Git stores the entire history of a project, it is easy to revert to a previous version in case of errors. Developers can also roll back specific commits or remove branches without compromising the project's stability.

Use Cases for Git

Git is used in a wide range of scenarios and development environments. Some of the main ones include:

- **Open-Source Projects**: Many open-source projects use Git for code management. Platforms like GitHub and GitLab allow developers from around the world to contribute easily by proposing changes through pull requests. Famous open-source projects that use Git include the Linux kernel, Node.js, and React.

- **Corporate Software Development**: Git is commonly used in companies for developing proprietary applications and software. Its flexibility and support for multiple branches allow teams to work on different features simultaneously without creating conflicts.

- **Documentation Management**: Git is not limited to just source code. It can also be used to version control documentation and other types of files. For example, it can be employed to manage technical manuals or specification documents.

- **Educational Projects**: Git is widely used in academic settings to teach versioning and collaboration. Universities and coding bootcamps often introduce Git as an essential tool for learning collaborative development practices.

Installing Git

System Requirements

Before proceeding with the installation of Git, it is important to ensure that your system meets the minimum requirements. Fortunately, Git is a lightweight tool and does not require particularly high resources.

- **Windows**: Git can be installed on all modern versions of Windows, starting from Windows 7. It is recommended to have at least 256 MB of RAM and a few hundred MB of free disk space.

- **macOS**: Git works on all recent versions of macOS. Generally, no special configurations are needed as macOS includes development tools that facilitate installation.

- **Linux**: Git is available on most Linux distributions and is officially supported on Ubuntu, Debian, Fedora, CentOS, and others. It is important to have access to your distribution's package manager for a simple installation.

Download and Installation on Windows

To install Git on Windows:

1. **Download the Installer**: Go to the official Git website (https://git-scm.com/) and download the latest version available for Windows.

2. **Run the Installer**: Once the file is downloaded, run the installer and follow the on-screen instructions. The process is fairly straightforward, but there are a few important options to keep in mind, including:

- **Default Text Editor**: Git will ask you to choose a default text editor. You can select your preferred editor, such as Vim, Notepad++, or Visual Studio Code.

- **System Path**: During installation, you will be asked if you want to add Git to your PATH. This option allows you to run Git commands from any Windows terminal.

3. **Complete Installation**: After the installation is complete, you can verify that everything is working correctly by opening Git Bash and typing `git --version` to see the installed version.

Download and Installation on macOS

Git can be installed on macOS in various ways:

1. **Xcode Command Line Tools**: The easiest method is to use Xcode's command line tools. Open the terminal and type:

```bash
xcode-select --install
```

This will install Git along with other development tools.

2. **Homebrew**: Another popular method is to use Homebrew, a package manager for macOS. If you already have Homebrew installed, you can install Git with the following command:

```bash
brew install git
```

3. **Official Installer**: You can also download the Git installer directly from the

official website (https://git-scm.com/) and follow the on-screen instructions.

Download and Installation on Linux

Git installation on Linux varies depending on the distribution. Here are some commands for common distributions:

- **Ubuntu/Debian**: Open the terminal and type:

    ```bash
    sudo apt update
    sudo apt install git
    ```

- **Fedora**: On Fedora, use the following command:

```bash
sudo dnf install git
```

- **Arch Linux**: On Arch Linux, you can install Git with:

```bash
sudo pacman -S git
```

- **Other Distributions**: For other distributions, consult the documentation for your package manager.

Initial Configuration

After installing Git, you need to configure

some basic settings, such as your username and email address. These will be associated with your commits.

1. **Set Username**: Open the terminal and type:

   ```bash
   git config --global user.name "Your Name"
   ```

2. **Set Email Address**: Type:

   ```bash
   git config --global user.email "your.email@example.com"
   ```

3. **Verify Configuration**: You can view all configuration settings by running:

```bash
git config --list
```

Other useful settings include choosing a default text editor for Git and configuring color for more readable output. For example, you can set the default editor with the following command:

```bash
git config --global core.editor "vim"
```

Git is now ready to be used on your system.

Conclusion

Git is a powerful and versatile tool for source code management and collaboration in software development. Its distributed architecture, advanced branch management, and speed make it an ideal choice for projects of any size, whether open-source or corporate. Installing and configuring it properly is the first step in fully leveraging its capabilities. Whether you're working on a project solo or collaborating with a team, Git simplifies the versioning process and enhances development productivity.

2.Fundamental Concepts of Git

Git is a distributed version control system that allows multiple developers to work together on a source code project without overwriting each other's work. It efficiently manages changes to the code, keeping track of every modification made. In this section, we will explore some fundamental concepts of Git, explaining how it works through practical examples.

Repositories and Projects

A repository (or repo) is the central structure around which the entire Git workflow revolves. A repository is simply a folder that contains all the files and directories related to a project, along with a hidden `.git` subfolder that stores all the Git information necessary to track changes. Every project managed with Git will have an associated Git repository.

A project can be considered as the collection of all the files and resources that make up the final output (e.g., a software application). Git allows you to version and track all changes to these files over time.

Example of Creating a Repository:

To create a new local repository, you can use the command:

```bash
git init
```

This command initializes a new Git repository in the current directory, creating the `.git` subfolder to track changes.

If you want to clone an existing remote repository (e.g., from GitHub), you can use:

```bash
git clone https://github.com/user/project.git
```

```

## Difference Between Local and Remote Repositories

A Git repository can be either local or remote. The main difference between the two is their location and how they are used in the Git workflow.

- **Local Repository**: This is a complete copy of the repository that resides on the developer's machine. This repository contains all the project files and the entire change history. Developers can perform operations such as commit, branch, merge, and others without needing to connect to the internet or a remote server.

- **Remote Repository**: A remote repository is a copy of the repository hosted on a remote server or a platform like GitHub, GitLab, Bitbucket, etc. It is accessible over a network and is used to synchronize work between various developers. The `push` and
```

`pull` operations are used to transfer changes between local and remote repositories.

Example of Linking Local and Remote Repositories:

To link a local repository to a remote repository, the `git remote add` command is used. For example:

```bash
git remote add origin https://github.com/user/project.git
```

Here, `origin` is the name assigned to the remote repository, and the URL is the path to the remote repository.

Commits and the Commit Tree

A commit in Git represents a snapshot of the project at a specific point in time. Each commit is a saved change that can include the addition, modification, or deletion of files. Git tracks every commit, allowing you to go back to any previous version of the project.

When you make a commit, Git creates a snapshot of all the tracked files. These snapshots are linked together to form a commit tree, which represents the project's history. Each commit has a unique identifier, called a hash (usually a SHA-1 hash), which allows you to refer to that specific commit.

Example of Commit:

After modifying a file and preparing the changes, you can create a commit using:

```bash
git commit -m "Commit description"
```

In this case, the `-m` option allows you to provide a descriptive message explaining the changes.

Viewing the Commit Tree:

To see the commit tree, you can use the command:

```bash
git log
```

This will show the entire commit history, including associated messages, authors, and hashes.

Branching and Merging

Branching is one of Git's most powerful features. A branch is a parallel line of development. For example, you can create a separate branch to work on a new feature or fix a bug without interfering with the main branch (often called `main` or `master`).

Merging is the process of integrating one branch into another. Once work on a branch is complete, you can merge it into the main branch, consolidating the changes.

Example of Creating a Branch:

To create a new branch called `new-feature` and switch to it:

```bash
git checkout -b new-feature
```

Example of Merging a Branch:

After completing the work in the `new-feature` branch, you can merge it into the main branch with:

```bash
git checkout main
git merge new-feature
```

```

## Tagging

Tagging in Git allows you to mark specific points in the project history with easy-to-remember labels. Tags are often used to mark release versions (e.g., `v1.0`, `v2.0`). There are two types of tags: annotated and lightweight.

- Annotated tags are full tags that include a message, author, and date.
- Lightweight tags are simple references to a specific commit.

### Example of Creating a Tag:

To create an annotated tag:

```bash
git tag -a v1.0 -m "Version 1.0"

```

Viewing Existing Tags:

To view the existing tags:

```bash
git tag
```

File Status and Repository Changes in Git

In Git, each file can be in one of the following states:

- **Modified**: The file has been changed, but the changes haven't been staged for commit.

- **Staged**: The file is ready to be committed.

- **Committed**: The file has been saved permanently in the project's history.
```

Example of Viewing File Status:

You can view the status of files in your repository using:

```bash
git status
```

Staging Files in Git

Staging is the process of preparing modified files for commit. In Git, files must be moved from the "modified" state to the "staged" state before they can be committed.

Example of Staging Files:

To add a modified file to the staging area, use the `git add` command. For example:

```bash
```

```
git add filename.txt
```

To add all modified files:

```bash
git add .
```

File Operations with Git

Git allows a variety of file operations such as deletion, moving, and renaming. These operations are tracked by Git and can be included in subsequent commits.

Example of Deleting a File:

To delete a file and track it in Git:

```bash
```

```
git rm filename.txt
```

Example of Renaming a File:

To rename a file:

```bash
git mv old_name.txt new_name.txt
```

Undoing Changes and Viewing History in Git

Git provides several tools for undoing changes or navigating the project's history. Some useful commands for managing these operations include:

- **git checkout**: Allows you to restore previous file versions or switch to another branch.

- **git reset**: Can be used to undo commits or remove files from the staging area.

- **git revert**: Creates a new commit that undoes the changes of a previous commit, while keeping the history intact.

Example of Undoing Changes:

If you've modified a file but haven't committed yet, you can undo the changes with:

```bash
git checkout -- filename.txt
```

To remove a recent commit:

```bash
git reset --soft HEAD^
```

Managing Remote Repositories

Managing remote repositories is one of the most common operations in Git, especially when working in teams. Some useful commands include:

- **git push**: Sends local changes to the remote repository.

- **git pull**: Fetches changes from the remote repository and integrates them into your local copy.

- **git fetch**: Retrieves changes from the remote repository without immediately merging them into the current branch.

Example of Pushing Changes:

After making a commit, you can push it to the remote repository with:

```bash
```

git push origin main
```

### Example of Pulling Changes:

To integrate changes from the remote repository:

```bash
git pull origin main
```

Tags and Aliases in Git

In addition to tags, Git allows you to create aliases to simplify frequent commands. Aliases can be configured via the `.gitconfig` file.

Example of Creating an Alias:

To create an alias that replaces `git status` with `git st`:
```

```bash
git config --global alias.st status
```

Conclusion

The fundamental concepts of Git, such as repositories, branches, commits, and tags, form the foundation for effectively working with this powerful distributed version control system. Knowing how to manage file status, staging operations, remote repositories, and project history allows you to fully master the Git workflow, making it an essential tool for every developer.

3. Basic Git Commands

Git is one of the most powerful and widely used tools for distributed version control, particularly in the field of software development. Effectively managing a Git repository requires familiarity with a series of basic commands that cover daily operations such as creating new repositories, cloning existing ones, tracking files, committing changes, and more. In this document, we will explore these fundamental commands with practical examples and detailed explanations, diving into each aspect with due attention.

Creating a New Repository

Creating a new Git repository is the first step in starting to track changes in a project. A **repository** is the structure that Git uses to store the project's change history. It can either be created from scratch or based on an existing project.

Command: `git init`

To start a new project with Git, use the `git init` command. This command creates a new Git repository in the current directory, generating a hidden folder called `.git` that contains all the necessary files to track changes.

Example:

```bash
mkdir git-project
cd git-project
git init
```

This will create a new folder named `git-project`, navigate into it, and initialize a new Git repository.

Expected output:

```
Initialized empty Git repository in /path/to/git-project/.git/
```

At this point, the repository is empty and ready to accept the project files.

Cloning an Existing Repository

Cloning a repository means downloading an exact copy of a remote repository (for example, from GitHub, GitLab, or Bitbucket) and creating a corresponding local repository. Cloning is useful when you want to contribute to an existing project or work with a shared repository among multiple developers.

Command: `git clone`

To clone a remote repository, use the `git clone` command followed by the URL of the repository you want to copy.

Example:

```bash
git clone https://github.com/user/project.git
```

In this example, Git will download a full copy of the remote repository from the GitHub server and create a new directory named `project`, containing all files and change history.

Expected output:

```
Cloning into 'project'...
remote: Counting objects: 100, done.
remote: Compressing objects: 100% (50/50),
```

done.
Receiving objects: 100% (100/100), 10 MiB | 1.0 MiB/s, done.
```

If you want to clone a repository into a directory with a different name, you can specify it as follows:

```bash
git clone https://github.com/user/project.git folder-name
```

Adding Files to the Repository

Git does not automatically track all files in your project directory. You need to explicitly specify which files you want Git to monitor
```

using the `git add` command.

Command: `git add`

The `git add` command adds files or changes to the **staging area**, which is an intermediate zone where files are "staged" before being committed.

Example - Adding a Single File:

```bash
git add filename.txt
```

This command will add `filename.txt` to the staging area, making it ready to be included in the next commit.

Example - Adding All Files:

```bash
git add .
```

```

This command will add all new or modified files in the current directory to the staging area.

Expected output:

No direct output is generated by the `git add` command, but you can verify the current status of the repository using `git status`.

---

### Committing Changes

A **commit** is one of the fundamental operations in Git. A commit represents a point in the project's history, including all the changes made to files in the staging area. It's like taking a "snapshot" of the current project state.
```

Command: `git commit`

To create a commit, you must first add files to the staging area (using `git add`), then you can use the `git commit` command to confirm these changes.

Example - Commit with Message:

```bash
git commit -m "Descriptive message of changes"
```

The `-m` flag allows you to include a commit message directly from the command line. This message should be brief but descriptive, explaining the changes made.

Example - Commit with Text Editor:

If you don't specify the `-m` option, Git will open the default text editor to enter the commit message:

```bash
git commit
```

Expected output:

```
[main 34b1a6c] Descriptive message of changes
 2 files changed, 10 insertions(+), 2 deletions(-)
```

Each commit is identified by a unique hash (in this case, `34b1a6c`).

Viewing the Repository Status

It's important to constantly have an overview of the repository's status to understand which files have been modified, which have been added to the staging area, and which have not. Git offers the `git status` command to display this information.

Command: `git status`

The `git status` command shows the current state of the repository, including changes that have been added to the staging area and those that are still untracked.

Example:

```bash
git status
```

Expected output (continued):

```
    modified:   file1.txt
```

Changes not staged for commit:

  (use "git add <file>..." to update what will be committed)

  (use "git restore <file>..." to discard changes in working directory)

        modified: file2.txt

Untracked files:

  (use "git add <file>..." to include in what will be committed)

        new-file.txt
```

In this example, `file1.txt` is ready to be committed, while `file2.txt` has been modified but not yet added to the staging area. `new-file.txt` is not yet being tracked by Git.

---
```

Undoing Changes

Git provides various ways to undo changes depending on what you need to do: discard untracked changes, remove files from the staging area, or reset a commit.

1. **Discarding Untracked Changes**

If you have modified a file but don't want to include those changes in the next commit, you can discard them and restore the file to its original state.

Command: `git restore`

To undo changes to a file that haven't been committed:

```bash
git restore filename.txt
```

This command restores the file to the state of the most recent commit.

Example:

```bash
git restore file1.txt
```

Expected output:

The file `file1.txt` will return to its previous state and will no longer be considered modified.

2. **Removing Files from the Staging Area**

If you've added a file to the staging area but don't want to include it in the next commit, you can remove it from the staging area with:

Command: `git restore --staged`

To unstage a file:

```bash
git restore --staged filename.txt
```

This command doesn't delete the changes to the file, it simply removes it from the staging area.

3. **Reverting to a Previous Commit**

If you've already committed changes but want to undo that commit, you can use:

Command: `git reset`

To undo the last commit while keeping the changes in the working directory:

```bash
git reset --soft HEAD^
```

```

This command will undo the most recent commit, but the changes will remain in your working directory and staging area.

If you want to completely discard the changes and reset everything to the previous commit:

```bash
git reset --hard HEAD^
```

These basic Git commands form the core of day-to-day operations with Git. The ability to create and clone repositories, add files and commit changes, view the repository status, and undo changes is essential for efficiently managing a project using Git. By becoming familiar with these commands and integrating
```

them into your workflow, you can use Git to track code versions, collaborate with other developers, and maintain organized project management.

Each command can be further explored and optimized with advanced options, but mastering these basic commands is the first step toward fully utilizing Git in a professional capacity.

4. Branch Management in Git

Branch management is one of the core aspects of Git, allowing developers to work on multiple lines of development within the same project. **Branches** let developers isolate their work, develop new features, fix bugs, or experiment with new ideas, while keeping the main branch stable until the changes are ready to be integrated.

In this document, we will explore various aspects of Git branch management, including branch creation, switching between branches, merging branches, resolving conflicts, and deleting branches, with practical examples for each operation.

What is a Branch?

A **branch** in Git is a movable pointer to a commit. Every project starts with a default branch, usually called `main` or `master`. Creating a new branch allows you to "diverge" from the main line of development, enabling you to work independently of the source code on other branches.

A branch contains a series of commits, and these can be modified without affecting other branches, making Git particularly powerful for managing complex projects or large teams.

Creating a New Branch

When working on a new feature or bug fix, it is often good practice to create a separate branch. This way, you can work without altering the code on the main branch (e.g., `main` or `master`).

Command: `git branch`

The `git branch` command allows you to

create a new branch. However, creating a branch doesn't automatically switch to that branch. To switch to the new branch, you'll need to use the `git checkout` or `git switch` command.

Example - Creating a New Branch:

Let's assume you're on a branch called `main` and want to create a new branch to develop a feature called "new-feature."

```bash
git branch new-feature
```

This creates a new branch called `new-feature`. However, you're still on the `main` branch. You can confirm this using:

```bash
git branch
```

```

Expected output:

```
  new-feature
* main
```

The asterisk indicates the current branch, which in this case is still `main`.

#### Creating and Switching Directly to a New Branch:

A more efficient way to create and immediately switch to a new branch is to use the `-b` option with `git checkout` or `git switch -c`.

```bash

git checkout -b new-feature
```

or, alternatively:

```bash
git switch -c new-feature
```

This command will create the branch and move you to it in a single step.

Expected output:
```
Switched to a new branch 'new-feature'
```

Switching Between Branches
```

Once you've created a branch, you need to know how to switch between available branches. Git makes this operation simple with the `git checkout` or `git switch` commands. Switching branches allows you to access the source code and commit history of that specific branch, leaving other branches intact.

Command: `git checkout` or `git switch`

`git checkout` is the most commonly used command to switch between branches, though `git switch` is a more modern way to change branches.

Example - Switching to an Existing Branch:

```bash

git checkout new-feature

```

or with `git switch`:

```bash
git switch new-feature
```

Expected output:
```
Switched to branch 'new-feature'
```

If you run the `git branch` command again, you'll see that the asterisk now indicates that you're on the `new-feature` branch.

```bash
git branch
```

Output:

```
* new-feature
  main
```

Now you're working on the `new-feature` branch, and all changes and commits you make will apply to this branch.

Merging Branches

One of the most common operations in Git is merging branches. After completing work on a separate branch (e.g., developing a new feature), you usually want to merge that branch into the main branch (`main`) to integrate the new changes into the primary project.

Command: `git merge`

To merge two branches, you use the `git merge` command. Before merging, you need to be on the branch where you want to integrate the changes. For example, if you want to merge the `new-feature` branch into the `main` branch, you should first switch to `main`, then execute the merge.

Example - Merging a Branch:

1. Switch to the `main` branch:

    ```bash
    git checkout main
    ```

    or with `git switch`:

```bash
git switch main
```

2. Merge the `new-feature` branch into the `main` branch:

```bash
git merge new-feature
```

Expected output:
```
Updating a2c24d2..b3f82d1
Fast-forward
 file1.txt | 10 ++++++++++
 1 file changed, 10 insertions(+)
```

Types of Merge:

1. **Fast-forward merge**: This type of merge occurs when there are no divergences between the two branches. Git simply moves the target branch pointer forward to the last commit of the branch being merged. This type of merge does not create a new merge commit.

2. **Merge with a merge commit**: When there are divergences between branches, Git will create a merge commit to combine the changes from both branches.

Resolving Merge Conflicts

Sometimes, when merging two branches, **merge conflicts** occur. This happens when Git is unable to automatically resolve differences between files modified in both branches. When this happens, you need to manually resolve the conflicts before completing the merge.

Example of a Conflict:

Suppose you've modified the same file (`file1.txt`) in both the `main` and `new-feature` branches. When you try to merge, Git won't be able to decide which version of the file to keep.

Running:

```bash
git merge new-feature
```

You might receive a message like this:

```
Auto-merging file1.txt
```

CONFLICT (content): Merge conflict in file1.txt

Automatic merge failed; fix conflicts and then commit the result.
```

#### Resolving Conflicts:

1. **Locate the conflicts**: Open the file flagged by Git (in this case, `file1.txt`). Inside the file, you'll see the conflicts highlighted like this:

   ```txt
   <<<<<<< HEAD
   Content from the main branch
   =======
   Content from the new-feature branch
   >>>>>>> new-feature
   ```

2. **Edit the file**: Resolve the conflict by
   ```

choosing which part of the code to keep or by manually merging both versions. For example:

```txt
Combined final content
```

3. **Stage the resolved file**: After resolving the conflict and saving the changes, you need to stage the file:

```bash
git add file1.txt
```

4. **Complete the merge**: Once all conflicts are resolved, commit the merge:

```bash
git commit
```

Deleting Branches

After completing work on a branch and merging it into the main branch, it's often a good idea to delete the branch to keep the repository clean and organized. This is particularly useful for temporary branches created for feature development or bug fixes.

Command: `git branch -d`

The `git branch -d` command deletes a local branch. Before deleting a branch, ensure all changes have been merged into the main branch or that you no longer need the branch.

Example - Deleting a Local Branch:

```bash
git branch -d new-feature
```

```

Expected output:

```
Deleted branch new-feature (was b3f82d1).
```

If you try to delete a branch that hasn't been merged, Git will show an error. If you're sure you want to delete the branch, you can force the operation using `-D`:

```bash
git branch -D new-feature
```

Deleting a Remote Branch:

If you want to delete a branch on a remote repository (e.g., on GitHub or GitLab), you can do so using the `git push` command with the `--delete` option.
```

Example:

```bash
git push origin --delete new-feature
```

Expected output:

```
To https://github.com/user/project.git
 - [deleted]         new-feature
```

Branch management is a fundamental part of the Git workflow. Creating branches helps keep code organized, fosters team collaboration, and simplifies the implementation of new features and fixes. Knowing how to create, switch between branches, merge, resolve conflicts, and delete branches is essential for using Git efficiently.

Branches provide a safe and controlled way to work on multiple features in parallel without interference. The concept of isolating and merging code allows teams to work independently while maintaining the integrity of the project on the main branch.

5. Managing Remote Repositories in Git

One of Git's most powerful features is its ability to manage remote repositories. A **remote repository** is a version of a project hosted on a remote server, accessible via the Internet or a local network. Remote repositories enable collaboration among multiple developers, allowing them to download (pull) and upload (push) changes to and from a remote server.

Managing remote repositories is crucial for distributed development teams, where multiple programmers work simultaneously on different aspects of the project. With Git, collaborators can work on their local machines and periodically sync with the remote repository to ensure they have the most up-to-date version of the project.

In this guide, we will explore how to manage remote repositories in Git, starting with adding them and moving on to advanced management of multiple remotes.

Adding a Remote

When working with Git, a local repository can be linked to one or more remote repositories. Adding a remote repository means specifying the URL of the repository hosted on a service such as GitHub, GitLab, Bitbucket, or a private server.

Command: `git remote add`

To link a remote repository to your local repository, use the `git remote add` command. You must provide a name for the remote (often called `origin` by convention) and the URL of the remote repository.

Basic Syntax:

```bash
git remote add <remote-name> <remote-url>
```

Example 1: Adding a Remote from GitHub

Let's say you have a local repository and want to link it to a remote repository hosted on GitHub. You can do this as follows:

```bash
git remote add origin https://github.com/user/project.git
```

In this example:

- `origin` is the name given to the remote repository. It's common practice to call the main remote repository `origin`, but you can use any name.

- The URL is the complete address of the remote repository.

Example 2: Adding a Remote via SSH

If you prefer using SSH (which is more secure and often preferred for long-term connections), you can add a remote with the SSH URL:

```bash
git remote add origin git@github.com:user/project.git
```

Verifying the Connection to the Remote

After adding a remote, you can check its

details using the `git remote -v` command, which shows a list of remotes with their URLs:

```bash
git remote -v
```

Expected output:

```
origin  https://github.com/user/project.git (fetch)
origin  https://github.com/user/project.git (push)
```

In this case, you'll see that the remote `origin` is associated with both the **fetch** (downloading changes from the remote) and **push** (uploading changes to the remote) operations.

Pushing and Pulling Changes

Once a remote repository is added, most interactions with it happen through two main commands: `git push` and `git pull`. These commands allow you to upload changes to the remote repository and download changes from the remote repository, respectively.

Pushing Changes

The `git push` command uploads commits from your local repository to a remote repository. It is generally used to sync local work with the remote, making your changes available to other collaborators.

Command: `git push`

The `git push` command accepts several options, but the basic syntax is:

```bash
git push <remote-name> <branch-name>
```

- `<remote-name>`: the name of the remote repository, which in our case is `origin`.
- `<branch-name>`: the name of the branch you want to push to the remote.

Example 1: Pushing the `main` Branch

Let's assume you've made some commits on the `main` branch and want to send them to the remote repository on GitHub:

```bash
git push origin main
```

```

This command will upload commits from the `main` branch of your local repository to the `main` branch of the remote repository `origin`.

#### Example 2: Pushing a New Branch

If you've created a new branch (e.g., `new-feature`) and want to push it to the remote for the first time:

```bash
git push origin new-feature
```

If the branch does not exist on the remote yet, Git will automatically create it.

Pulling Changes
```

If you're working on a project and want to update your local `main` branch with the latest changes made by other developers, you can use the `git pull` command to download and merge those changes into your local repository.

Example 1: Pulling Changes from the `main` Branch

```bash
git pull origin main
```

In this example:

- `origin` is the name of the remote repository.

- `main` is the branch from which you want to pull the changes.

When you run `git pull`, Git will download all the changes made by other developers on the remote `main` branch and attempt to merge them into your local `main` branch. If there are conflicts, you will need to resolve them manually (as described in the section on merge conflicts).

Example 2: Pulling a Specific Branch

If you are working on a branch other than `main`, such as `new-feature`, and you want to download the latest changes from the remote repository:

```bash
git pull origin new-feature
```

This command pulls the changes made to the `new-feature` branch from the remote repository `origin` and merges them into the `new-feature` branch in your local repository.

Cloning from a Remote Repository

The `git clone` command is one of the most commonly used when starting to work on an existing project. This command allows you to create a local copy of a remote repository, including all the files, commit history, branches, and repository configurations.

Command: `git clone`

The basic syntax for cloning a remote repository is:

```bash
git clone <remote-url>
```

This command downloads the remote repository into the directory where you run it. You can also specify a destination directory if you want the cloned copy to be created in a different location.

Example 1: Cloning a GitHub Repository

Let's say you want to clone a project from GitHub. The command to do this is:

```bash
git clone https://github.com/user/project.git
```

This command creates a complete copy of the `project` repository on your computer. Once cloned, you can explore the commit history, create new branches, make changes, and sync them with the remote repository.

Example 2: Cloning a Repository via SSH

If you've set up SSH to access remote repositories (e.g., on GitHub), you can clone a repository using the SSH URL:

```bash
git clone git@github.com:user/project.git
```

This command works just like the HTTPS URL but uscs SSH authentication, often preferred for a secure connection and to avoid entering your password each time.

Example 3: Specifying a Destination Directory

If you want to clone the repository into a different directory than the default (usually the repository name), you can specify a destination directory:

```bash
git clone https://github.com/user/project.git my-project
```

In this case, the repository will be cloned into a folder called `my-project`.

Managing Multiple Remote Repositories

In some scenarios, you may need to manage multiple remote repositories for a single project. For instance, you may have a primary remote repository on GitHub and another on

Bitbucket, or you may want to collaborate with multiple teams that use different remotes.

Git allows you to manage multiple remotes by assigning each one a unique name. You can then use these names to perform `push`, `pull`, and `fetch` operations from each remote repository.

Adding Another Remote

To add a second remote, use the `git remote add` command, just as you did for the first remote. However, this time, you'll assign a different name to the second remote.

Example 1: Adding a Second Remote from Bitbucket

Let's say you already have a repository on GitHub added as `origin`, and now you want to add another repository on Bitbucket:

```bash
git remote add bitbucket https://bitbucket.org/user/project.git
```

In this case, we're adding a new remote called `bitbucket`.

Verifying Remotes

After adding multiple remotes, you can verify which remotes are associated with your local repository using the command:

```bash
git remote -v
```

Expected output:

```
origin   https://github.com/user/project.git (fetch)
origin   https://github.com/user/project.git (push)
bitbucket https://bitbucket.org/user/project.git (fetch)
bitbucket https://bitbucket.org/user/project.git (push)
```

Pushing to Multiple Remotes

Once you have multiple remotes configured, you can choose which remote to push your changes to. To push to a specific remote, simply specify its name.

Example 1: Pushing to GitHub (`origin`)

If you want to push changes to the GitHub repository:

```bash
git push origin main
```

Example 2: Pushing to Bitbucket (`bitbucket`)

To push the same changes to Bitbucket:

```bash
git push bitbucket main
```

This flexibility allows you to keep multiple remote repositories in sync and share your code with different teams or platforms.

Fetching from Multiple Remotes

Similarly to pushing, you can fetch changes from a specific remote:

Example 1: Fetching from `origin` (GitHub)

```bash
git fetch origin
```

Example 2: Fetching from `bitbucket` (Bitbucket)

```bash
git fetch bitbucket
```

```

The `fetch` command downloads changes from the remote without automatically merging them, giving you a chance to review the changes before deciding to incorporate them.

---

## Renaming and Removing Remotes

If you ever need to rename or remove a remote repository, Git provides simple commands to manage this.

### Renaming a Remote

To rename a remote, use the `git remote
```

rename` command:

```bash
git remote rename <old-name> <new-name>
```

Example: Renaming `bitbucket` to `bb`

```bash
git remote rename bitbucket bb
```

This changes the remote name from `bitbucket` to `bb`.

Removing a Remote

To remove a remote repository, use the `git remote remove` command:

```bash
git remote remove <remote-name>
```

Example: Removing the `bitbucket` Remote

```bash
git remote remove bitbucket
```

This command removes the `bitbucket` remote from your local repository configuration.

Managing remote repositories is an essential

part of working with Git, especially when collaborating on projects with others. By mastering commands like `git remote add`, `git push`, `git pull`, and `git clone`, you'll be able to efficiently sync your local work with remote repositories and contribute to projects hosted on platforms like GitHub, Bitbucket, and GitLab.

With the ability to manage multiple remotes, you can collaborate on complex projects that involve multiple teams or deployment targets, giving you flexibility in how you handle your code.

6.Workflow and Best Practices in Git

Git is a powerful tool for source code management, but effective use depends on understanding key concepts and following best practices. In this guide, we will explore branching models, common workflows like Git Flow, how to write frequent commits and effective commit messages, the use of `.gitignore` files, and tools and interfaces for Git. We will also dive into branching, merging, rebasing, and advanced Git tools like stash, cherry-pick, bisecting, and submodules.

Git Branching Model

Git's branching model allows you to work on multiple versions of a project simultaneously without affecting the main code. Branches enable you to develop new features, fix bugs, and experiment without compromising the stability of the main project.

Key Concepts

1. **Main Branch (`main` or `master`)**: This is the main project branch and contains the stable production code. Traditionally named `master`, many projects now use `main` to better reflect its purpose.

2. **Development Branch**: Used to develop new features. It can be created from the main branch and merged back when ready.

3. **Feature Branch**: Created to work on a specific feature. It is usually branched off the development branch.

4. **Bugfix Branch**: Used to isolate bug fixes. It can be branched from the main or development branch, depending on the severity of the bug.

5. **Release Branch**: Created when a new version of the software is ready for release. This branch allows for testing and minor fixes before releasing.

6. **Hotfix Branch**: Created to fix urgent issues in production. It is usually branched off the main branch and then merged into both the main and development branches once the problem is solved.

Example of Branching Model

Suppose you have a repository with the main branch `main`. You want to add a new feature and fix a bug.

1. **Create a Development Branch**

    ```bash
    git checkout -b development
    ```

2. **Create a Feature Branch**

   ```bash
   git checkout -b feature-new-feature
   ```

3. **Create a Bugfix Branch**

   ```bash
   git checkout -b bugfix-error-fix
   ```

4. **Create a Release Branch**

   ```bash
   git checkout -b release-1.0
   ```

5. **Create a Hotfix Branch**

   ```bash
   ```

```
git checkout -b hotfix-urgent-fix
```

This way, you can work on different aspects of the project in parallel, keeping the code organized and easily manageable.

Git Flow Workflow

Git Flow is a popular branching model that helps organize the workflow in a software project. It defines a set of branches and strategies to manage software development and release.

Key Concepts of Git Flow

1. **Main Branch (`main` or `master`)**:

Contains the stable production code. All releases are tagged on this branch.

2. **Development Branch (`develop`)**: Used for integrating new features and improvements. It serves as the base for all feature branches.

3. **Feature Branch**: Created from the development branch to work on a new feature. Once completed, it is merged back into the development branch.

4. **Release Branch**: Created from the development branch when preparing for a new version release. It allows testing and minor fixes before the release.

5. **Hotfix Branch**: Created from the main branch to fix urgent issues in production. It is merged into both the main and development branches.

Git Flow Workflow Example

1. **Starting a New Project**

   - Create the main branch `main`.

   - Create the development branch `develop`.

2. **Create a New Feature**

   ```bash
   git checkout develop
   git checkout -b feature/feature-name
   # Develop the feature and commit changes
   git checkout develop
   git merge feature/feature-name
   ```

3. **Prepare a New Release**

   ```bash
   git checkout develop
   ```

```
git checkout -b release/1.0
# Run testing and make minor fixes
git checkout main
git merge release/1.0
git tag 1.0
git checkout develop
git merge release/1.0
```

4. **Handle a Hotfix**

   ```bash
   git checkout main
   git checkout -b hotfix/1.0.1
   # Fix the issue
   git checkout main
   git merge hotfix/1.0.1
   git tag 1.0.1
   git checkout develop
   ```

    git merge hotfix/1.0.1

```

Git Flow is effective for projects with well-defined release cycles and teams working on multiple aspects of the project simultaneously.

---

## Lesson on Frequent Commits

Frequent commits are a fundamental Git best practice. Each commit represents a snapshot of the project at a specific point and helps maintain a detailed history of changes.

### Benefits of Frequent Commits

1. **Easier Debugging**: With frequent commits, you can easily isolate changes that
```

introduced bugs and revert to a previous state if necessary.

2. **Manageable Code**: Frequent commits help keep the code manageable and reduce the risk of complex conflicts.

3. **Work Documentation**: Each commit documents the work done and the changes made, providing a clear history of the project's progress.

Example of Frequent Commits

Suppose you are working on a feature and making changes in different stages. You can commit at each significant stage:

1. **First Stage: Add a New Feature**
   ```bash
   git add file1 file2
   ```

git commit -m "Added new search feature"
```

2. **Second Stage: Fix an Issue**

   ```bash
   git add file3

   git commit -m "Fixed issue with search module"
   ```

3. **Third Stage: Refine the Code**

   ```bash
   git add file4

   git commit -m "Refactored search code"
   ```

By committing frequently, you ensure that every change is documented and easily reversible if needed.
   ```

Writing Effective Commit Messages

Commit messages are crucial for understanding the project's history and the reasons behind changes. Well-written commit messages help keep the code organized and facilitate collaboration.

Guidelines for Writing Effective Commit Messages

1. **Be Clear and Concise**: The commit message should clearly explain the change in a concise manner.

2. **Use the Imperative**: Write the message as if you are giving a command, e.g., "Add feature X" instead of "Added feature X."

3. **Describe the Why, Not Just the What**: Explain why the change was made and what problems it solves.

4. **Separate the Header and Body**: If the commit message requires a longer description, use a blank line to separate the header from the body.

Example of Commit Messages

1. **Simple Commit**

    ```bash
    git commit -m "Add data validation"
    ```

2. **Commit with Detailed Description**

    ```bash
    git commit -m "Add support for data
    ```

validation"

```



```

Added data validation to the registration form to ensure that

user input is correct before submission.

- Check that required fields are not empty
- Validate that email is in the correct format
```

---

## Using `.gitignore` Files

The `.gitignore` file is used to specify which files or directories Git should ignore. This is useful for excluding temporary files,
```

environment-specific configuration files, and other files that should not be versioned.

Creating and Configuring a `.gitignore` File

1. **Create the `.gitignore` File**

   Create a file named `.gitignore` in the root of your repository.

2. **Add Rules to the `.gitignore` File**

   Specify the patterns of the files and directories you want to exclude. Here is an example `.gitignore` file:

   ```
   # Ignore log files
   *.log

   # Ignore temporary files directory
   ```

/tmp

Ignore IDE configuration files
.idea/
*.suo
```

In this example, log files, the `/tmp` directory, and IDE configuration files are excluded from Git.

3. **Apply the Changes**

After adding rules to the `.gitignore` file, Git will stop tracking the matching files. However, files already tracked won't be ignored until you remove them from the repository.

```bash
git rm --cached file-to-ignore.log

```

Git Tools and Interfaces

Git can be used through the command line, but there are also several graphical interfaces and IDE integrations that make working with Git easier.

Command-Line Interface

The command-line interface is the primary tool for working with Git. It provides detailed control over all operations and allows you to run complex commands.

Basic Command Examples
```

1. **Clone a Repository**

    ```bash
    git clone https://github.com/user/project.git
    ```

2. **Create a New Branch**

    ```bash
    git checkout -b feature/feature-name
    ```

3. **Push Changes**

    ```bash
    git push origin main
    ```

4. **Pull Changes**

    ```bash
    git pull origin main
    ```

```

5. **View Repository Status**

   ```bash
   git status
   ```

6. **View Commit History**

   ```bash
   git log
   ```

Git GUI Tools

Graphical interfaces for Git offer a more visual and often more intuitive experience than the command line. Some popular tools include:
   ```

Sourcetree

Sourcetree is a free Git client that provides a graphical view of repositories, branches, and commits. It simplifies complex Git operations and is ideal for beginners.

GitKraken

GitKraken is a powerful Git GUI client with an intuitive interface and extensive features. It provides visual representations of Git operations and integrates with popular repositories like GitHub and Bitbucket.

IDE Integrations

Most modern integrated development environments (IDEs), such as Visual Studio Code, JetBrains products, and Eclipse, have built-in Git support. This allows you to perform Git operations without leaving your coding environment.

Branching, Merging, and Rebasing

Branching, merging, and rebasing are essential concepts for managing parallel development in Git.

Branching

Branching allows you to create separate lines of development within a repository. Each branch represents an independent version of the project. You can use branches to develop new features, fix bugs, or prepare for releases without affecting the main project.

Merging

Merging combines the changes from one branch into another. This is commonly used when a feature branch is completed and needs to be integrated into the main or development branch.

Example of Merging

1. Create a new branch and make changes:

   ```bash
   git checkout -b feature/new-feature
   # Make changes and commit
   git add .
   git commit -m "Add new feature"
   ```

2. Merge the branch into the main branch:

   ```bash
   git checkout main
   git merge feature/new-feature
   ```

3. Push the changes to the remote repository:

   ```bash
   git push origin main
   ```

Rebasing

Rebasing is an alternative to merging that rewrites the commit history of a branch. It moves your changes to the tip of another branch, resulting in a cleaner project history.

Example of Rebasing

1. Create a new branch and make changes:

```bash
git checkout -b feature/new-feature
# Make changes and commit
git add .
git commit -m "Add new feature"
```

2. Rebase the branch onto the main branch:

```bash
git checkout feature/new-feature
git rebase main
```

3. Push the changes to the remote repository:

```bash
git push origin feature/new-feature
```

Advanced Git Tools

Git provides several advanced tools to handle complex scenarios in development.

Git Stash

`git stash` is used to save changes that you are not ready to commit. It allows you to switch branches or work on other tasks without committing partial changes.

Example of Using Git Stash

1. Stash your changes:

   ```bash
   git stash
   ```

2. Switch branches and work on something else.

3. Retrieve your changes later:

   ```bash
   git stash apply
   ```

Git Cherry-Pick

`git cherry-pick` allows you to apply individual commits from one branch to another. It's useful when you want to apply specific fixes without merging an entire branch.

Example of Using Git Cherry-Pick

1. Find the commit hash you want to cherry-pick:

```bash
git log
```

2. Apply the commit to the current branch:

```bash
git cherry-pick <commit-hash>
```

Git Bisect

`git bisect` helps you find the exact commit that introduced a bug by performing a binary search through the commit history.

Example of Using Git Bisect

1. Start bisecting:

   ```bash
   git bisect start
   ```

2. Mark the current commit as good or bad:

```bash
git bisect bad
git bisect good <last-known-good-commit>
```

Git will automatically check out commits, and you can continue marking them as good or bad until you find the problematic commit.

Git Submodules

Git submodules allow you to include one repository inside another. This is useful for managing dependencies and modular projects.

Example of Using Git Submodules

1. Add a submodule to your repository:

```bash
git submodule add https://github.com/another-project.git
```

2. Initialize the submodule:

```bash
git submodule init
```

3. Update the submodule:

```bash
git submodule update
```

Effective use of Git is crucial for managing software projects. By following the branching models, workflows like Git Flow, and best practices like frequent commits and clear commit messages, you can improve collaboration and maintain project organization. Tools like `.gitignore`, Git stashing, cherry-picking, bisecting, and submodules further enhance your ability to handle complex scenarios in development.

7. Automation and Continuous Integration with Git

Automation and continuous integration (CI/CD) are essential for ensuring that software is developed and released efficiently and with high quality. Git, as a version control system, plays a crucial role in these processes, especially when integrated with CI/CD tools and platforms like GitHub. In this chapter, we will explore how to configure Git with CI/CD, use webhooks with GitHub, and how Git fits into the DevOps practices. Additionally, we will see how to use GitHub to create and manage repositories, collaborate on open-source projects, and manage pull requests and issues.

Configuring Git with CI/CD

Continuous Integration (CI) and Continuous

Deployment (CD) are practices that automate the process of testing and distributing code. Configuring Git for continuous integration can vary depending on the tools and platforms used. Here we will explore a general configuration example with GitHub Actions, one of the most popular CI/CD tools.

GitHub Actions

GitHub Actions is an automation platform that allows you to create CI/CD pipelines directly within GitHub. It enables you to automate builds, tests, and deployments, and integrates tightly with GitHub repositories.

Steps to Configure GitHub Actions

1. **Create a Configuration File**

   GitHub Actions workflows are defined in YAML files located in the

`.github/workflows` directory of the repository. For example, let's create a file called `ci.yml` to configure a continuous integration workflow.

```yaml
# .github/workflows/ci.yml
name: CI Pipeline

on:
  push:
    branches:
      - main
  pull_request:
    branches:
      - main

jobs:
  build:
```

```
    runs-on: ubuntu-latest

    steps:
    - name: Checkout code
      uses: actions/checkout@v2

    - name: Set up Node.js
      uses: actions/setup-node@v2
      with:
        node-version: '14'

    - name: Install dependencies
      run: npm install

    - name: Run tests
      run: npm test
```

In this example, the workflow runs whenever a push or pull request is made to the `main` branch. The workflow performs the following steps:

- Checkout the code.

- Set up Node.js.

- Install the project dependencies.

- Run the tests.

2. **Test the Workflow**

After adding the configuration file, commit and push it to the repository:

```bash
git add .github/workflows/ci.yml
git commit -m "Add CI workflow"
git push origin main
```

GitHub Actions will automatically start the defined workflow and display the results in the "Actions" section of the GitHub repository.

3. **Monitor the Results**

You can monitor the workflow execution and results directly in the "Actions" tab of your GitHub repository. Each workflow run is logged, and you can view details for each step.

Using Webhooks with GitHub

Webhooks are a way for applications and services to communicate with each other. In GitHub, webhooks can be used to send repository events to an external server, enabling custom integrations and automation.

Configuring a Webhook

1. **Access Repository Settings**

   Go to the "Settings" section of your GitHub repository.

2. **Add a Webhook**

   In the "Webhooks" section, click on "Add webhook."

3. **Enter the Webhook URL**

   Enter the URL of your server that will receive the notifications. This server must be able to handle POST requests sent by GitHub.

```plaintext
https://example.com/webhook
```

4. **Select Events to Send**

Choose which events will trigger the webhook. You can choose to receive notifications for all events or only specific ones like push events, pull requests, or issues.

5. **Configure Security**

You can add a secret to ensure that the webhook requests are secure and actually come from GitHub.

6. **Test the Webhook**

After configuring the webhook, you can test it to ensure it works correctly. GitHub provides an option to send a test event to your server.

Git and DevOps

DevOps is based on closer collaboration between development and operations, and Git is a fundamental part of this process. Git helps ensure effective source code management, facilitating versioning and collaboration.

Git in the DevOps Lifecycle

1. **Continuous Integration (CI)**: Git enables developers to integrate code changes into a central repository, where CI tools like GitHub Actions or Jenkins can automate builds and testing.

2. **Continuous Deployment (CD)**: Git facilitates the continuous deployment of software. Changes in the repository can automatically trigger deployment to staging or production environments.

3. **Monitoring and Feedback**: Git allows the integration of monitoring tools to gather feedback on code in production, improving the feedback loop and continuous improvement.

4. **Automating Operations**: With Git, you can automate the build, testing, and deployment process using scripts and CI/CD tools, reducing the risk of human errors and speeding up software releases.

Using GitHub

GitHub is a platform based on Git that offers advanced features for managing repositories, collaboration, and version control. We will explore how to create and manage repositories on GitHub, collaborate on open-source projects, manage pull requests and code reviews, and handle issues.

Creating an Account on GitHub

1. **Sign Up**

   Go to [GitHub](https://github.com) and click "Sign up." Complete the registration form by entering your username, email, and password.

2. **Set Up Your Account**

   After creating the account, follow the

instructions to configure your preferences and, if needed, set up your profile and security settings.

Creating and Managing Repositories on GitHub

1. **Create a New Repository**

   - Go to your GitHub homepage.

   - Click "New repository."

   - Fill out the form with the repository name, a description (optional), and choose whether to make it public or private.

   - Click "Create repository."

2. **Clone a Repository**

You can clone a GitHub repository to your local machine using the `git clone` command:

```bash
git clone https://github.com/user/repo.git
```

3. **Managing a Repository**

Once a repository is created, you can manage it using Git and GitHub's web features:

- **Add and Commit Changes**: Use Git commands to add and commit changes.

- **Push and Pull**: Sync your local repository with the remote one using `git push` and `git pull`.

- **Manage Branches and Tags**: Create and manage branches and tags using both Git commands and the GitHub interface.

Collaborating on Open Source Projects

GitHub is an excellent platform for contributing to open-source projects. Here's how you can collaborate:

1. **Fork a Repository**

   - Go to the open-source repository on GitHub.

   - Click "Fork" to create a copy of the repository in your account.

2. **Clone the Forked Repository**

   ```bash
   git clone https://github.com/your-username/forked-repo.git
   ```

3. **Make Changes and Submit a Pull

Request**

- Create a new branch for your changes:

    ```bash
    git checkout -b new-feature
    ```

- Make your changes and commit them:

    ```bash
    git add .
    git commit -m "Added a new feature"
    ```

- Push the modified branch:

    ```bash
    git push origin new-feature
    ```

- Go to the forked repository's page on GitHub and click "Compare & pull request" to submit a pull request to the original repository.

Pull Request and Code Review

Pull requests are a way to request that your changes be reviewed and merged into the main repository. Here's how to manage them:

1. **Create a Pull Request**

   - After submitting a modified branch, go to GitHub and click "Pull requests."
   - Click "New pull request" and select the branch with the changes.
   - Add a description and click "Create pull request."

2. **Code Review**

   - The repository maintainers will review the pull request, comment on the code, and may request further changes.

   - Respond to comments and make changes as necessary.

3. **Merge the Pull Request**

   - Once approved, the pull request can be merged into the main branch.

   - Click "Merge pull request" and confirm the merge.

Issue Management

Issues on GitHub help track bugs, feature requests, and other tasks.

1. **Create a New Issue**

   - Go to the "Issues" section of your repository.

- Click "New issue" and fill out the form with the title and description.

2. **Managing Issues**

   - Assign issues to team members.

   - Label and organize issues for easier tracking.

   - Use comments to discuss the issues and provide updates.

3. **Closing Issues**

   - Once the issue is resolved, you can close it manually from the issues page.

This comprehensive overview of automation, continuous integration, and the use of GitHub should give you a thorough understanding of how Git and GitHub can be used to optimize the development and code management process. Whether you're working on a personal project, collaborating on open-source efforts, or implementing DevOps practices, these tools and techniques will help you improve efficiency and quality in your work.

Index

1. Introduction to Git pg.4

2. Fundamental Concepts of Git pg.21

3. Basic Git Commands pg.37

4. Branch Management in Git pg.53

5. Managing Remote Repositories in Git pg.71

6. Workflow and Best Practices in Git pg.94

7. Automation and Continuous Integration with Git pg.125

www.ingramcontent.com/pod-product-compliance
Lightning Source LLC
Chambersburg PA
CBHW050257230526
45471CB00005B/1915